I0828917

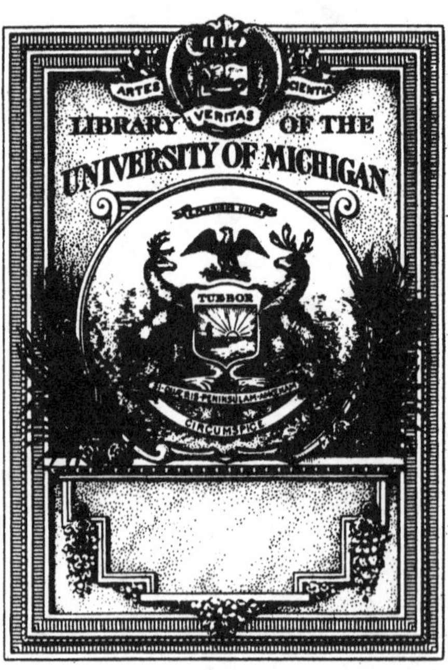
ARTES
VERITAS
SCIENTIA
LIBRARY OF THE
UNIVERSITY OF MICHIGAN
TUEBOR
CIRCUMSPICE

THE CRIME COMMISSION OF NEW YORK STATE

Crime commission

A STUDY OF 201 TRUANTS IN THE NEW YORK CITY SCHOOLS BY THE SUB-COMMISSION ON CAUSES AND EFFECTS OF CRIME

1927

ALBANY
J. B. LYON COMPANY, PRINTERS
1928

CRIME COMMISSION

CALEB H. BAUMES, Chairman
BURTON D. ESMOND, Vice-chairman

B. ROGER WALES
WALTER S. GEDNEY
DAVID S. TAYLOR
THOMAS S. RICE
WM. LEWIS BUTCHER
JANE M. HOEY
JOHN KNIGHT
JOSEPH A. McGINNIES
GEORGE F. CHANDLER

HERBERT L. SMITH, Secretary
Senate Chamber, Albany

SUB-COMMISSION

WM. LEWIS BUTCHER, Chairman
JANE M. HOEY
JOSEPH A. McGINNIES

ASSISTANTS

RAYMOND R. MOLEY
Research Advisor

HARRY M. SHULMAN
Research Worker

A REPORT TO THE COMMISSION OF THE SUB-COMMISSION ON CAUSES AND EFFECTS OF CRIME

To the Crime Commission of New York State:

The Sub-Commission on Causes and Effects of Crime herewith submits a report containing findings and recommendations based on a study of 201 truants in the New York City schools.

All of which is respectfully submitted as a partial report of the work allocated to this Sub-Commission.

Dated, February 28, 1927.

WM. LEWIS BUTCHER, *Chairman.*
JANE M. HOEY,
JOSEPH A. MCGINNIES,
Sub-Commission.

A STUDY OF 201 TRUANTS IN THE NEW YORK CITY SCHOOLS

Introduction

It is a striking fact, corroborated in the Crime Commission's study of men now in State's Prisons, that the criminal of today was in too many cases, the truant of yesterday. That does not mean, of course, that every child who is today a truant will become a criminal to-morrow, but that the chances are the criminal group will undoubtedly be recruited more in proportion from the truant group than from the non-truant group. In view of this fact, it is timely that attention be paid to the causes of truancy, to the present day treatment, and to a plan for future treatment of the problem.

The child who remains away from school for a few days during a term either because of illness or indisposition, or because of some special occasion, is not the subject of this study. Many children are occasionally truant because of some such trifling reason, frequently to serve the convenience of their parents. Such cases total hundreds of thousands yearly. This large group of casual truants is unimportant despite its large size, because it reflects no basic attitude toward school life. There is, on the other hand, a small persistently truant group of children which comes to the attention of the Children's Court and the Hearing Division of the Bureau of Attendance.

These are children in whom a definite attitude of dislike or even of disgust toward school has been built up. This group has been regarded by school teachers and administrators as more or less of an enigma, because these children stand out so decidedly from their playmates as being free from the domination of school discipline. Threats, punishment, hearings at the Bureau of Attendance, pleas of parents, frequently even commitments to the truant school do not seem to be successful in breaking up this attitude of unyielding resistance to compulsory schooling. It is because the truant is usually such an enigma to the average school administrator that he arouses so much ire. The response of the school administrator to the problem of truancy takes very little cognizance of the specific factors which have entered into the individual case of truancy. His response is in terms of an established tradition.

The New Problem of the Truant

There was a time when the problem of truancy was not serious because there was no serious interest in enforcing compulsory attendance. Three decades ago, a child who was disinclined to attend school, disinterested or ungovernable, was politely but firmly expelled from the system. There was no formality attached to his going. He was told to leave and never to come back. It was not necessary to secure working papers in order to work, or Health

Department certificates, nor parent's consent, nor employer's guarantee of a job. Things were delightfully free and easy. The truant was thrown out and remained out.

He became somewhat of a hero to the neighborhood group of "goody-goody" children who still continued to go to school. He would frequently come back to the school yard, and hanging around in front of the building with some of his pals, would make contemptuous remarks about teachers as they passed, or deride the other children as they came out for recess, on their enforced thralldom. The essential point here is that several decades ago the child's resistance to a system resulted in victory for the child.

Today, all this has changed. Compulsory education has been established as a habit in the minds of most parents and practically all children. The moment a child stays away from school an Attendance officer is at his door making inquiry into the case of the absence. Several unauthorized absences result in a report being transmitted to the Hearing Department of the Bureau of Attendance. The child is placed upon probation. If he violates his probation he is frequently sent to the Truant School, or if his parents refuse to sign the consent blank entitling the Bureau of Attendance to commit him, he is brought into the Children's Court on a charge of delinquency. At the present time, in other words, the persistent truant is up against the cold facts of a system that is hard to beat—one that does not solve its problems by ignoring him, but by paying persistent attention to him.

A system that is inflexible, running squarely into a resistance that is unyielding, is bound to result in a personality distortion of some sort in the child who is fighting the system. This clash of wills inevitably results in an attitude of resentment on the part of the child toward a system that he fails to understand. This resentment, we believe, is one of the roots from which develop strong anti-social tendencies exhibited in the attitude of most criminals.

A study on truancy, published in June, 1915, by Elizabeth A. Irwin, field worker of the Committee on Hygiene of School Children, of the Public Education Association, gave certain very interesting conclusions on 150 children, with regard to the questions of causation, of present treatment and of a plan for future handling of the problem.

The Bureau of Attendance of the New York City Board of Education recognized the need for individual treatment of truants as outlined in this report and in the next few years several diagnostic studies were made on small groups of truants. In 1915 a small number of truants had the benefit of examinations conducted at the clinic of the College of the City of New York. This group consisted of 56 cases. Half of the group was found to be mentally defective.

During the same year thorough medical examinations of truant children in the Second Attendance District, covering the area between 14th and 59th streets, the East and North rivers, were given. The health of the truant group was found to be decidedly bad. The statistics on their state of health was compared with the Board of Health records on unselected school children who were examined in 1912. This comparison shows the tremendous physical handicaps under which these truants suffered. Thus, only 2.9 per cent of normal school children were suffering from malnutrition, whereas 26.2 per cent of truants were undernourished. Seven and three-tenths per cent of normal school children had defective vision, whereas 20.1 per cent of truants were so handicapped. Forty-nine and four-tenths per cent of normal children had defective teeth, whereas 91.2 per cent of truants had bad teeth.

Physical examinations were conducted among truants on a still larger scale during 1917–1918. Between 75 per cent and 85 per cent of the truants were discovered to have serious physical defects. In 1916 and 1917 children were referred to the educational clinic of the College of the City of New York for psychological diagnosis and diagnosis of educational handicaps. In 1919 and 1920 the National Committee for Mental Hygiene, in co-operation with the Bureau of Attendance, conducted a piece of experimental work with probationary school boys in Yorkville.

The encouraging initial efforts made since 1915 have come to naught, however, through failure of the Board of Education to make provisions for extension of the work on a larger scale, or to provide permanent facilities and a budget for this work, even on a small scale. There is today no permanent program for the individual social treatment of truant children in New York City. Because of this situation the Sub-Commission on Causes has undertaken an original study of its own and has compared its findings and conclusions with those of the Public Education Association.

A Study of 201 Persistent Truants

This study of truancy has been made possible through the splendid co-operation of the Bureau of Attendance of the New York City Board of Education. The schedules were drawn up by the Sub-Commission on Causes and the clerical work of preparing all of the tables was done by the Bureau of Attendance. This study consists of an analysis of 201 cases, chosen at random from those who have been persistent truants during 1926. The material was gathered by means of a questionnaire which was filled out by the attendance officers, from information obtained from the children themselves, from their parents, from the teachers, and from school records. The total number of children committed as truants during 1926 was 626. The number committed during 1926 is about average, therefore, the group of cases studied represents one-third of the total group committed to the Truant School during any year, and may therefore be regarded as an adequate sampling of cases. This group was chosen from the group of pending commitments and represents only children in the Borough of Manhattan.

Home Status of Truants

An important factor in the problem of truancy is the home status of the truant child. Tabulations unfortunately tell very little of the factors involved in each situation. The following tables, however, do reiterate certain well-known facts even though they throw no new light on the home status of the truant.

Is the home life normal, in a broad sense? Are both parents living, or is one parent dead? Are the parents living together or are they separated? These questions are vital because they are directly concerned with the matter of daily supervision in the home. Where the father is dead, the mother usually has to work during the day to provide at least part of the family income. Complete subsidization has seldom been the policy of philanthropic societies in such cases. Where the mother is dead, an older sister may assume prematurely the family responsibilities, or the children may be boarded with relatives or even with strangers. In any case, haphazard, indifferent or incompetent supervision takes the place of the daily, interested supervision of the average mother.

Where the family is a broken one, due to desertion, separation, or because of commitment of either parent to an institution, inadequate supervision has been often complicated by divided authority, a result of clashes between the parents. The child who has been the victim of turbulent home scenes usually does not accept the authority of the remaining parent with docility. He is torn between two allegiances and often chooses to go his own path, determined to cut loose and be "on his own" as soon as possible. In any case, the authority of the remaining parent is undermined.

What then were the home conditions of the 201 boys who awaited commitment to the truant school? The following table tells the story:

Marital Conditions

Both parents dead	5	
Father dead	37	
Mother dead	18	
Broken home due to death	60	30%
Family deserted by father	3	
Family deserted by mother	1	
Parents divorced	1	
Parents separated	20	
Father in institution	4	
Mother in institution	1	
Father in prison	2	
Broken home, incompatibility	**32**	**15%**
Normal	**109**	**55%**

Comparison with Children's Court Figures

A comparison of the home status of the foregoing with that of children brought into the Children's Court during a four-year period is valuable since delinquency has been ascribed so frequently to lack of proper home supervision. The probation department of the court, in the annual report made to the chief justice, gives among other social data the following figures on parental condition among boys on whom home investigations were made:

	1921 %	1922 %	1923 %	1924 %	*Average* %
Normal home, parents together	65	67	67	65	66
One parent dead.....	23	21	20	19	21
Both parents dead....	3	2	2	3	2
Parents separated	6	5	6	7	6
Miscellaneous	3	5	5	6	5

Whereas, only 55 per cent of our group had normal homes, 66 per cent of all the delinquent boys coming to the Children's Court over a four-year period had normal homes.

Miss Irwin, in her truancy study, sought the facts on the same conditions. She found that only 26 per cent of her group of 150 truants came from homes which she termed as being "economically normal." However, most of her cases came from one West side section in Manhattan, noted for its large proportion of broken homes, whereas our own group represent a borough-wide selection.

We have unfortunately no measure of the extent to which broken homes figure in the normal non-truant school population of the same cultural and economic status as the group we have studied. Such a measure would be indeed valuable, but would require careful selection of samples, to ensure equivalent groups.

Because we lack data on a control group, we can make no comparative statement on the matter of home break-down, but can say that a seemingly high percentage of truants come from broken homes.

Parental Economic Status

There probably was a time when boys were truant because their illegal employment was regarded as necessary to maintain the family. Today, regardless of parental attitude on this matter, the strictness of the Bureau of Attendance and the Employment Certificating Division of the Board of Education, as well as of factory inspection, has made it well-nigh impossible for the young truant to spend his free time at lucrative employment. Of our own group of 201 cases, only 10 spent their time while truant in working, 5 peddling papers, 1 peddling candy and 4 working on wet-wash laundry wagons.

The tendency of minors not to be wage-earners is shown in the table which follows. In the 201 families studied, the minors under

18 made no contribution in 133 cases, and made total contributions under $20 per week in 58 more cases. In only 10 families did minors under 18 contribute more than $20 a week, and in 9 out of these 10 families the total family income was above $60 a week, well above the average, indicating that some form of business enterprise was providing the minors with occupations, instead of street trades.

It would seem to be a safe generalization that children are seldom if ever truant because of illegal employment. However, the economic status and occupation of the father has a force and a subtle influence in no way related to the activities of the children while truant, but directly related to their attitude toward education in general. Children whose parents either have a good general education or whose occupation has required special training are undoubtedly given constant reminders of the advantages of schooling. The child whose father is unskilled can usually acquire a "drive" toward education only if his father constantly emphasizes his own handicaps through lack of schooling, and has ambition for a better occupation for his son. While it is true that many parents have this broad view, it is equally true that a great many do not, and their children are content to drop from school into employment without planning of any sort.

Occupations of Parents

In the 201 cases studied, the occupations of 162 living fathers were obtained. Of this group, 95 worked at jobs that required no education, hardly even literacy. Only 23 had jobs requiring education of any sort, such as high school or trade school, and of these only one had a position requiring higher education.

These facts might be cited by the casual reader to prove that some direct relationship exists between truancy and parental occupation. Actually, no general conclusions can be drawn, as we have no reliable data on the relative proportion in the general population of the same economic status as our truant group, of laborers and of more highly trained workers. For all we know, parents of non-truants of the same economic status might be found to fall into identical occupation groups as parents of truants.

Reasons Assigned for Lack of Parental Control

In 147 out of 201 cases, officers of the Bureau of Attendance familiar with the children and the homes gave their estimates of the reasons for loss of parental control. These estimates are not the result of careful study by trained case workers, but they are interesting to note even though allowances must be made for their possible inaccuracy. Certain obvious factors of neglect were most emphasized. Thus, in 70 cases, absence of either parent, because of death or separation, or because of employment, was stressed as the prime factor in lessening of parental control.

Table Showing Income of Families of 201 Truants

Weekly Income of	Total	Under $25	25–30	30–35	35–40	40–45	45–50	50–55	55–60	60–65	65–70	70–75	75–80	80–85	85–90	90–100	100–110	Over 110	Not given
Total	201	19	19	19	24	21	22	19	7	8	11	8	4	2	1	2	5	4	6

Table Showing Contributions to Total Income In Families of 201 Truants by Minors under 18

Family Income		Under $25	25–30	30–35	35–40	40–45	45–50	50–55	55–60	60–65	65–70	70–75	75–80	80–85	85–90	90–100	100–110	Over 110	Not stated
No contributions	133	17	18	16	16	13	16	11	2	5	4	3	1	2	0	0	2	1	6
Under $15	30	1	...	2	8	2	2	6	1	1	2	2	2	...	...	1	...	...	...
15–20	28	1	1	1	...	5	4	2	1	1	4	2	1	...	1	1	1	2	...
20–25	2	...	...	...	...	...	...	...	1	...	...	1	...	...	...	...	...	...	...
25–30	3	...	...	...	...	1	...	...	...	...	1	...	...	...	...	...	1	...	...
30–35	3	...	...	...	...	...	...	...	1	1	...	...	...	...	...	...	1	...	...
35–40	1	...	...	...	...	...	...	...	1	...	...	...	...	...	...	...	...	...	...
55–60	1	...	...	...	...	...	...	...	...	...	...	...	...	...	...	...	...	1	...

In 37 cases, the parents are blamed as being indifferent, indulgent or weak. In 36 cases, the children were reported as being beyond parental control because of outside influences.

Parental Control—Lacking Because Of—

A.	Broken Family—	
	Father works—no mother	12
	No father—mother employed	30
	No father—mother unable to control	17
	Father employed out of city	2
B.	Both parents employed	7
C.	Beyond parental control	24
D.	Leniency of mother	14
E.	Example of older brothers	1
F.	Influences outside home (associates)	12
G.	Religious differences of parents	3
H.	Father drunkard—mother weak	2
I.	Indifference or laxity of parents	21
J.	Father works at night—sleeps during day	2
		147

In a majority of the cases, therefore, the parents through some circumstances, resulting from economic, or social maladjustment or personality deficiency, were inadequate to the task of controlling their children, according to the Attendance Officers.

To summarize the preceding findings, we may say that a high proportion of these truants came from homes that are broken, that most of them had fathers who are unskilled laborers, and that in the majority of the cases it was the opinion of the Attendance Officers that parental control was lacking.

Against these conclusions may be cited the facts that we do not know whether or not the proportion of broken homes is higher among truants than among non-truants of the same social status, whether the parents of non-truants stand relatively higher in the occupation scale, and if parental control among non-truants is relatively better.

The sober truth is probably that we do not know what weight the environmental factors have in production of truancy, nor will we know until control groups of normal children are studied and restudied.

The Individual Truant

Having considered the home environment, let us discuss the child himself. What of him? What has he to contribute to the reasons for his truancy? What of his mentality? What of his physical stamina? What of his degree of success in school life? Unfortunately, we cannot give an answer to the questions of mental and physical capacity as New York City does not study her truants closely. No clinical examinations of any sort are given to truants at the present time. The problem is treated purely from a disciplinary point of view and the repressive or negative method of treatment is used in preference to the more enlightened modern method of case study.

In 1915, after the conclusion of Miss Irwin's Truancy Study, the chief recommendation made by the Public Education Association was that thorough clinical examinations be given to truants. Twelve years have elapsed since that time, yet no thorough forward step has been taken despite the increasing availability in the community of clinical facilities and the increasing practice of adjusting behavior problems through case study rather than through repressive means.

We have, therefore, no data as to the intelligence or physical condition of the truant child. Miss Irwin, in her study, was able to report on this phase of the problem. Psychological examinations given to her group of truants showed that 43% of the children were feeble-minded, 49% of them were normal, and 8% were border-line in intelligence. The amount of subnormality which she discovered in her truancy group, therefore, was approximately twenty times as great as we would find in the normal child population. This, of course, is of tremendous significance, showing that among nearly one-half of the truant group the problem of truancy undoubtedly results from the child's inability to grasp the materials of the school curriculum. It is true of course that a great many of the more obviously defective children are examined by the Department of Ungraded Classes of the Board of Education and where it is deemed wise they are recommended for transfer to special classes. However, there are untold numbers of children of the less obvious, high grade moron, type of mental disability who do not come to the attention of the ungraded class of psychologists, yet who present distinct problems of maladjustment to the school curriculum and show this maladjustment in their obstinate refusal to attend school.

There is among truants, as among delinquents in general, a great deal of school retardation. This school retardation is in part a corollary of the large amount of feeble-mindedness to be found among the truant group but almost an equal amount of school retardation is to be accounted for on grounds of disinterest rather than inability. A recent study by Dr. Alexander Tendler, "Measurable Factors of Adjustment in Juvenile Delinquents—1925," made on a group of delinquents, who were approximately normal in intelligence showed several years of school retardation among this group despite the fact that practically all of the children had sufficient mental capacity to be in the proper grade.

Though the factors contributing to school retardation are many, the results upon the child are probably similar. The child who is kept back term after term, either for misconduct or lack of ability to learn ordinary academic subjects, loses his hope and his initiative. He sees his friends forge ahead, taking up new subjects, getting nearer to graduation, whereas he is doomed to a repetition of old studies taught in precisely the same way each time. He is the big boy in the class of small children. It is no wonder that rather than be daily reminded of his failure, that this type of pupil absents himself from school.

The extent to which the truants in our own group are retarded in school, is shown in the following table:

XIV–A

Table Showing Distribution of 186 Children by Number of Terms Taken to Reach Grade and Aggregate Number of Terms Retarded Before Compulsory Action Became Necessary

Number terms taken to reach present grade	Normal number terms to reach grade	1A		1B		2B		2B		3A		3B		4A		4B	
				1		2		3		4		5		6		7	
	Pupils	Terms retarded	Pupils	Terms retarded	Pupils	Terms retarded	Pupils	Terms retarded	Pupils	Terms retarded	Pupils	Terms retarded	Pupils	Terms retarded	Pupils	Terms retarded	Pupils
1																	
2																	
3	1	2	1														
4																	
5	1														1		
6	7							3	1	2	2	1	2		2		
7	6									3	1	2	1				3
8	8									4	1	3	2	2	1	1	2
9	10											4	1	3	1	2	1
10	12													4	1	3	2
11	14													5	3	4	3
12	18													6	1	5	2
13	23															6	1
14	24																
15	21															8	1
16	19																
17	13																
18	6																
19	2																
20	1																
Median — terms retarded of total retarded group in grade								3		2½		2		5		4	
Total number truants grade 1									1		4		7		10		15

Number terms taken to reach present grade	Normal number terms to reach grade	5A		5B		6A		6B		7A		7B		8A		8B		9A	
		8		9		10		11		12		13		14		15		16	
	Pupils	Terms retarded	Pupils	Terms retarded	Pupils	Terms retarded	Pupils	Terms retarded	Pupils	Terms retarded	Pupils	Terms retarded	Pupils	Terms retarded	Pupils	Terms retarded	Pupils	Terms retarded	Pupils
1																			
2																			
3	1																		
4																			
5	1																		
6	7																		
7	6																		
8	8		1		1														
9	10	1	1		5		1												
10	12	2	2	1	5		2												
11	14	3	1	2	1	1	4		2										
12	18	4	4	3	4	2	4	1	2				1						
13	23			4	1	3	6	2	6	1	8		1						
14	24	6	1	5	4	4	5	3	5	2	8	1	1						
15	21	7	1	6	3	5	1	4	5	3	2	2	3	1	3		2		
16	19					6	6	5	2	4	3	3	4	2	2				2
17	13	9	1	8	3	7	1	6	2	5	2					2	4		
18	6									6	1	5	4	4	1				
19	2					9	1	8	1										
20	1									8	1								
Median — terms retarded of total retarded group in grade		4		4		3		3		2		3		1½		2			
Total number truants grade 1			12		27		31		25		25		14		6		2	2	

It will be noted that the group of 201 truants has been separated according to the school grades of the children in the group. Thus, in grade 3–A, there were two truants who were retarded two terms, one three terms and one four terms (Table XIV–A, read the column from top to bottom. In grade 8, one truant was at grade, one was one term retarded and two who were retarded two terms (read down to the bottom of the column). The number of children who were at grade or above grade in the different terms have been set off from the lower portions of the column by being enclosed in boxes. It will be seen at a glance, therefore, that twenty-three of the 201 truants were at or above grade, one being above grade and twenty-two being at grade, and 178 truants were below grade. The median amount of retardation among the retarded group is to be found at the bottom of each column. It will be seen that the greatest amount of retardation is to be found among the pupils in the 4th and 5th grades, from 4–A through 5–B. This great amount of retardation probably represents that due to mental defect, as the feeble-minded pupils usually begin to reach their maximum level in about the 4th and 5th grades. The retardation among the truants in the upper grades, from 6th to 8th is seen to be somewhat less. This amount of retardation probably represents the more nearly normal group. However, even among the pupils whom we shall for the time being assume as the normal group, there is a sufficient amount of retardation to be quite disheartening. In the 6–B and 7–B terms for example, the median amount of retardation is three terms and there are some pupils who have been left back as much as six, seven, eight and nine terms. The despair that must enter the soul of a child after nine successive failures is incalculable in the mind of an adult.

The last series of figures in this table shows how the group of 201 pupils are distributed according to grade. It will be seen that truancy is most marked among the children in the 5th, 6th and 7th grades. In other words, persistent truancy takes time to develop and is most prevalent among the older children in the school. Considering the fact that the majority of these truants in the 5th, 6th and 7th grades are from two to four terms retarded they must be, therefore, on the average from one to two years older than the average child in the grade. Though normal children in the grades from 5–A to 7–A would be from 10 to 12 years old; in our truant group we would expect to find the average to be from 11 to 14 years of age. In other words, in the grades in which there is the most truancy we have many children who are beginning to approach the time of school graduation, who see themselves hopelessly retarded and for whom the ideal of education as exemplified in some type of high school or trade training has become shattered. Add to this the despair due to repeated failures, and it is not difficult to see why this group should be the most truant.

Of course, the only solution for this problem is a careful analysis of the reasons for retardation within each individual truant. As we have stated, one major factor would be that of mental incapacity. The other major factor is that of lack of interest. Since we have no information as to whether lack of interest in the specific case has origin in disability or in environmental factors, the best we can do is cite the tables indicating the school likes and dislikes and the school abilities and disabilities, of this truant group. The first table answers the question "At what is he skillful?"

At What Is He Skillful?

A. Nothing in particular	101
B. Plumbing	3
C. Carpentry	7
D. Drawing	7
E. Shoemaking	1
F. Playing cornet	1
G. Shop work	35
H. Carpentry and tinsmithing	1
I. Athletic games	4
J. Sheet metal work	5
K. Printing	4
L. Typewriting	1
M. Arithmetic	1
N. Reading	3
O. Spelling	1
P. Penmanship	2
Q. Spelling and history	1

In 101 cases the answer is "nothing in particular." In other words, in 50% of our cases the children show no ability in their ordinary daily work that would throw any light upon their vocational or even their academic preference. In 35% of the cases the boys were considered as being skillful in shop work. In 33 other cases they were considered skillful in some other form of manual activity, such as plumbing, carpentry, shoemaking, and sheet metal work, and in only 8 cases were they considered proficient in subjects requiring facility in abstract portions of the curriculum, such as spelling, reading, etc. Our truant group therefore consists partly of a group that is not proficient in anything and partly of a group that is proficient in some form of hand work. Here we have another basis of maladjustment, as the ordinary school curriculum does not provide much outlet for the child who is gifted manually. The boy who is skilled at shopwork for example, must go through twenty-two hours a week of school drudgery in arithmetic and history in order to obtain three hours a week of a subject in which he has some capacity. The final word on this problem must of course be said by educators,

but it would seem to a layman that the truant child requires an adjustment of the curriculum to meet his special needs.

In the next table is answered the question "For what school work has he a special dislike?"

For What School Work Has He a Special Dislike?

A.	All school work	38
B.	Arithmetic	43
C.	History	22
D.	Geography	36
E.	Reading	10
F.	Spelling	9
G.	Algebra	1
H.	Biology	1
I.	Writing	1
J.	Grammar	14
K.	Shop work	1
L.	Drawing	2

Thirty-eight of the 201 truants dislike all school work. Forty-three dislike arithmetic, 22 history, 32 geography, 14 dislike grammar, only one dislikes shop work and two dislike drawing. They show no dislike for manual subjects, like shop work and drawing because they have capacity for shop work and drawing. They utterly dislike arithmetic, history, geography and grammar because they have no capacity for these subjects as is shown in the preceding table. In other words, that which is known to be a sound psychological truth is here demonstrated, that interest goes with capacity and disinterest goes with incapacity. The problem is whether we shall force the truant to fit the curriculum or fit the curriculum to meet the capacities and handicaps of the truant and non-truant retarded child. Modern psychology has thoroughly demonstrated that capacities are more or less innate and not to be created. From our point of view it would seem therefore, that the attempt to force any child to fit the routine curriculum is to force him in the direction of a personality distortion that is bound to end disastrously.

We have so far considered the child with regard to his home supervision and with regard to his school maladjustment. It is frequently forgotten that the child lives in a social world of his own, that creates a gap between home and school and of which very little is known by adults. It can not be emphasized too much that the social aspect of the child's life must not be neglected. The case study method too often neglects this phase of the child's life, the phase that to the child himself is probably most important. The question, therefore, arises as to whether in addition to the negative factors of lack of home supervision and lack of adjustment to school curriculum, there were not any other positive factors that were luring the child away from school. The first answer to this question is given in the following table on the "Incidents causing first truancy."

Incident Causing First Truancy

A.	Likes to roam streets	7
B.	Dislike for school	37
C.	Bad associates	77
D.	Absent because of illness — no wish to return	2
E.	"Left back" in school	1
F.	Went to "movies" with friends	6
G.	Wanted to go to work	12
H.	Went to park with friend	2
I.	Went fishing in Hudson river	1
J.	Was late for school	6
K.	Employment of mother	8
L.	Change of school — dislike for new one	7
M.	Dispute with teacher	3
N.	Fear of punishment in school	4
O.	Absence of teacher	1
P.	Went to fly pigeons	3
Q.	Inability to keep up with class	1

From this table it will be seen that in only the minority of the cases did the first truancy relate back to a school situation; 37 of the children had a generalized dislike for school. One was truant because he was left back in school, 6 because they were late for school, 7 because of a change in school, and a dislike for the new school, 3 because of a dispute with the teacher, 4 because of fear of punishment in school, 1 because of absence of teacher, 1 because of inability to keep up with class. Thus, 59 first truancies were related back to some school situation and 142 were related to some situation outside of the school. This material is of course not to be regarded as absolutely authentic since it is a more or less introspective account, but it has a certain value, coming as it does from the children themselves. Of the group of 141 cases where truancy had originated outside of the school scene, 77 cases were attributed to so-called bad associates. This we fear is a term used by Attendance officers and not by children. Children do not talk of "bad associates." However, the point is stressed that in a very large number of cases the children had a social life of their own whose influence lead them to do more pleasant things than going to school. What the nature of this social life is, may best be gleaned from the following, most interesting tabulation, "What is done by the truant while he is away from school."

Description of Diversions When a Truant

A.	Shoots craps	23
B.	Roaming streets, docks and yards	56
C.	Selling papers	5
D.	Goes to movies	18
E.	Goes to park	8
F.	Playing cards	5
G.	To park and playing craps	4
H.	Collecting junk to sell	5
I.	Riding in subway and "L"	10
J.	To movies and flying pigeons	7
K.	Stays at home	3
L.	To parks and movies	3
M.	Flying pigeons and shooting craps	5
N.	To movies and shooting craps	14
O.	Peddles fruits	1
P.	Stays in candy store	1
Q.	To movies and auto riding with older boys	2
R.	Flying pigeons and riding on wagons	3
S.	Delivering wet wash	4
T.	Stealing lead pipe and other things	5

It will be observed that practically all of the children do things while truant that require company. Illegal occupations are not stressed strongly in this tabulation. Commercial amusement, however, is stressed a good deal. In 44 out of 201 cases or approximately 20% of the group, the movies are stated to be one of the places where they spend their time while truant. This indictment of commercial recreation as a large factor in encouraging truancy supports the findings of other studies made by this sub-commission.

The last question that concerns us is, whether the truant child has already become a juvenile delinquent. Of the 201 cases studied, 38 had already been delinquents and had been so classified by the Children's Court, but 163 had not yet been found delinquent. In other words, although a proportion of these truant children had already presented other behavior problems serious enough to warrant court action, the majority of them were still in a pre-delinquent state. Whether all of them will become delinquent or whether none of them will become delinquent is only a matter for conjecture. The ordinary controls of social life will probably enter to check many of them from a delinquent career. Many others will undoubtedly join the ranks of court probationers and court commitments. The one conclusion we can draw from this final set of facts, is that we have in the truant group children whose anti-social attitude is as yet only reflected in their avoidance of an unpleasant task, namely going to school. There is yet time to attempt therapeutic work. This naturally brings us to the question of the numbers for whom such therapeutic work is necessary and the means that should be provided. The following table shows the number of children who have been committed for truancy since the organization of the Bureau of Attendance.

NUMBER OF CHILDREN COMMITTED FOR TRUANCY SINCE ORGANIZATION OF BUREAU OF ATTENDANCE

	Total	Director	Original commitments		Account violation of parole
			By Children's Courts	By Magistrates' Courts	
Total	8,171	6,828	1,177	166	2,979
School Year					
1914–15	553	351	202	....	88
1915–16	574	461	113	....	215
1916–17	624	543	81	....	256
1917–18	593	516	77	....	274
1918–19	584	451	133	....	227
1919–20	588	509	79	....	211
1920–21	643	579	64	....	280
1921–22	827	728	66	33	280
1922–23	729	624	76	29	328
1923–24	849	742	78	29	321
1924–25	640	542	63	35	214
1925–26	626	502	103	21	201
Sept. 1926 to Feb. 7, 1927	341	280	42	19	8

It will be noted that the total number has remained more or less constant since the first commitments in 1915 with the exception of a rise between 1921 and 1924. The figures show that the problem amounts roughly to handling each year, six or seven hundred children for whom ordinary controls have ceased to serve.

RECOMMENDATIONS FOR TREATMENT

In the light of our study it would seem that the truant requires consideration from several angles. His intelligence, educational activities and aptitudes require the study of clinical psychologists. His emotional attitudes toward home, toward school, toward his playmates and toward his life plan, require the study of physiatrists. A practical solution for his individual difficulties requires the co-operation of a staff of trained social workers. His physical condition, on which we have little or no information, certainly needs the close scrutiny of physicians. Finally, the school administrator must be called into conference with these other experts, for an adaptation of the school program to meet the needs of these children.

These various techniques resolve themselves into the component elements of mental hygiene clinics. Such clinics are needed and should be established in the school systems of this State, particularly for the study of truants and non-truant problem children. These clinics, in our opinion, should preferably be established in the school systems, rather than be organized as separate agencies, inasmuch as their purpose is to meet only the needs of school children. Again, by being established within public schools, these clinics will serve as educational centers for the teaching staff, as well as therapeutic centers for the pupils.

The trend of thought in the Board of Education of New York City at the present time is toward providing probationary schools where problem children may be segregated, and be given various clinical examinations and treatment. The Sub-Commission on Causes, however, feels that more effective work can be done by providing clinical treatment under normal, every day school conditions rather than under institutional conditions developing from a process of segregation of children presenting problems.

The recommendations of the Sub-Commission on Causes of the New York State Crime Commission therefore, are:

1. The establishment within the school system of clinics for the medical, psychological and phychiatric study of children presenting behavior problems.

2. That the school curriculum be revised to meet the needs of the large group of children who have not the capacity for ordinary academic training, due to defective mentality or emotional instability.

3. The two foregoing recommendations should be subjected to a careful analysis and evaluation by some competent agency either within or without the school system. Such a study should be undertaken soon after the initiation of the projects themselves.

4. The Bureau of Attendance, of the New York City Board of Education, should be provided with trained case workers, assigned limited case-loads, for the supervision of children who are persistently truant, or who present other behavior problems.

5. The funds necessary for the establishment of the facilities described in the four previous recommendations should come preferably from public sources, but should there be hindrances to the prompt availability of public funds, then it is strongly urged that generous private funds be made available for the initiation of these projects.

www.ingramcontent.com/pod-product-compliance
Lightning Source LLC
LaVergne TN
LVHW011138110826
845150LV00008B/2385